27 · 102

CW00403019

Contents

ALAMY/ GETTY

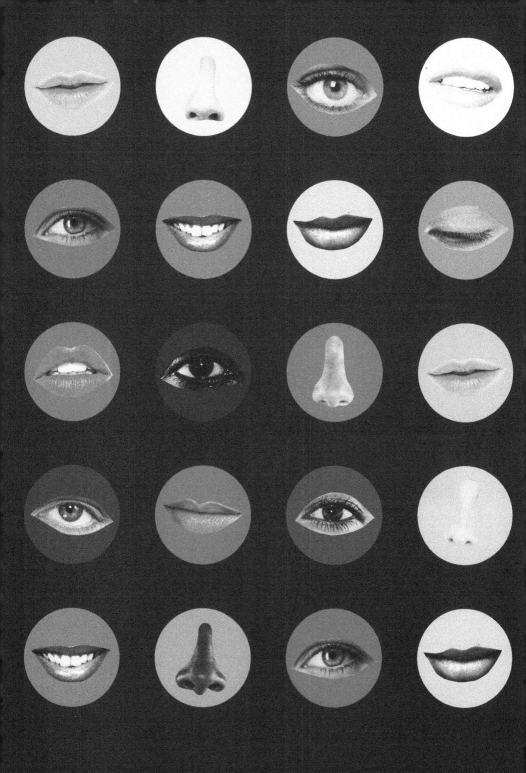

Chapter one

Professor Becky Francis on ability grouping and setting

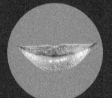

Becky Francis is director of the UCL Institute of Education and was previously professor of education and social justice at King's College London. Her research has been highly influential in policy and in schools, touching on school quality, gender and social justice in education. She is also one of the world's leading researchers into attainment grouping and setting. In this interview, she focuses on the last, explaining what the research suggests is the best approach for schools.

How much do we know about the impact of setting, attainment grouping and mixed-attainment grouping in schools?
One of the long-standing areas of international research is on different methods of grouping young people. The international research is very clear that overall, there is no positive impact of setting and streaming on young people's attainment. That's because, for the bigger group of higher-attaining kids, there's a tiny benefit to be put in top sets, whereas for the smaller group of low attainers in bottom sets and streams, there is a more substantial negative effect of being put in a lower-attainment group.

There is an important social justice angle to this for you, isn't there?
Kids come to school with different levels of what is known in the field as school readiness. Kids from disadvantaged backgrounds are already behind when they arrive in the early years at school. It's no surprise, then, that where schools practise attainment grouping, we find disproportionate amounts of kids from poor socio-economic backgrounds in low sets and streams.

And we know that kids in low sets and streams make poorer progress compared to the kids in higher sets and streams. So,

those kids are actually subject to a double disadvantage, which is being pushed on to them by our education system.

The very kids that might need the best help and the best practice, we know, are being disadvantaged by grouping practices that they're subject to at school. That is why it's an issue of social inequality.

One of the things that we've never known is whether the poorer [performance of lower-set pupils in terms of progress] can be explained simply by a self-fulfilling prophecy – the message kids get that they're "thick"

ALL IMAGES GETTY

practices that we know are associated with low sets and streams? For example, teachers with less subject expertise being put with those low groups, misallocation – which has been frequently documented – and so on.

It gets into a slightly contentious area, doesn't it? Teacher quality is a difficult issue to discuss. There is certainly a perception that schools give the most effective teachers to the top set and the set aiming for what was grade C. Is there anything in the research that suggests this is true?

Shockingly, there is, especially in the American literature. There are very clear associations with set level and what they would refer to as teacher effectiveness.

The notion of teacher quality or teacher effectiveness is very controversial and debated. Key indicators are usually taken to be level of subject qualification, length of time in teaching, experience and so on.

Against these measures, the literature has been quite clear, certainly in the United States, that there is a very strong association with the most experienced and expert teachers being put with the high sets.

We have also recently modelled this in relation to our English study and found the same tendencies.

Again, in terms of social justice, social injustice and, actually, basic equality of opportunity, we would say that, for kids in those low sets and streams, there's something going badly wrong for them.

or not good enough by putting them in what is frequently, actively referred to by teachers as a low-attainment group. Think of the message that gives, to the teachers and students, about their potential, and whether it's worth bothering and engaging.

You mean in terms of how the child sees themselves and also what the teacher believes they are capable of?

Exactly. Are those things working together for a self-fulfilling prophecy or might the poorer progress be due to some of the

Is there an association between those teachers in lower sets and behaviour issues, too? The perception is that lower sets are "naughtier".

If you put all your badly behaved kids in the bottom set, of course that set is going to have behavioural issues. Interestingly, the literature has shown that other factors than attainment do have an impact on who gets put in the low-attainment groups. You might not necessarily be put there simply because you're low attaining; there may be other issues as well.

Clearly, the research suggests that there are many issues with setting. Are these negative impacts amplified the earlier a child is set?
I don't think we know the answer. Certainly, I'm not familiar with studies that have tracked this systematically, longitudinally.

Nevertheless, we would certainly hypothesise that there would be a cumulative effect and that's something we've been looking at in my Education Endowment Foundation-funded study.

We've been looking at this over two years because we assume there will be a cumulative effect. What's very interesting is that there is increasing evidence about a real shift in practice in primary schools, even in the earliest years, with increased attainment grouping, often with the notion of these attainment tables. Within class grouping, that is really predominant in primary schooling now.

We had designed our project to be looking at kids starting secondary school in Year 7, imagining that, at least for the majority, they'd be being put in sets for the first time.

Actually, we found that quite the reverse is the case. The vast majority of kids in our study, certainly those that we've actually interviewed in focus groups, have already had experiences of attainment grouping in primary school.

There is a desperate need for research that starts with schools and with kids in primary schools in the early years and then tracks them through.

What about the other side of this, then: mixed-attainment teaching. Is there evidence to say that it is better?
Although there's this wealth of research, literature and evidence around setting and streaming, and what is referred to in the US as tracking, there's incredibly little research on mixed-attainment practice.

This is really important, because if we're not able to tell teachers what the alternatives look like and be able to provide really good-quality materials, support and so on, why on earth would they feel able to discard their practices of a lifetime and turn to something radically different without the research evidence?

I guess a lot of teachers will say it's easier to teach in a set. The range of attainment is narrower. Is that actually true? Is it more difficult to differentiate in a mixed-attainment group than a set?
I don't think the answer is clear. It's a commonly made point but, nevertheless, a valid one, that every class is a mixed-attainment group. You've always got that spectrum, particularly, where there is sloppy practice in setting that starts to look a little bit more like streaming – for example, where kids are set according to maths and then put in the same sets for science and so on.

One of the things that we see around the debate in this country is quite polarised positions, depending on people's backgrounds. Often they've either had experiences with setting and streaming, or with mixed-attainment practice, and [that informs] these arguments about whether one is easier and more effective than another from a teaching perspective.

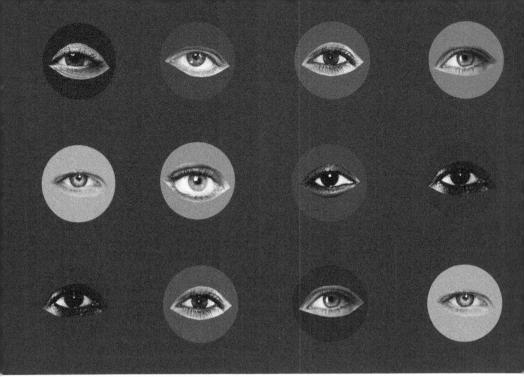

One of the fears that we've picked up in our project is that this mixed-attainment practice would exacerbate teachers' workload, which obviously we don't want and teachers don't have the capacity for. The system's creaking at the seams already. And there's a risk of almost creating three different lessons within a class, and that's not good practice in mixed attainment.

Has your study or research around it thrown up any best practice around mixed-attainment teaching?
The best practice that we have observed, within and outside of our study, involves starting at the top and then scaffolding back to ensure different attainment points and exit points for every child in the class. And, actually, I think that, if that approach is habitual and developed across a teaching team – your English department, your maths department and so on – this can

be enormously effective and shouldn't necessarily have to create more work.

But I think starting from scratch and overturning long-held cultural departmental habits is, of course, a big undertaking. So, if we want to see any change, then we – whether it's researchers, whether it's system leaders – have a duty to be providing the exemplars that teachers need for that.

But is it really just a workload issue? It might be controversial to say, but do some teachers think, "oh, I can really engage with my subject if I'm top set, I can really get some good conversations going. I don't really want to be doing the more basic stuff with the bottom set"?
It's a really good point. There is evidence of teachers being rewarded by being placed with the high sets and streams from the UK, in our study, and from the wider literature in the US as well. Interestingly, we found that

more senior teachers were more likely to be teaching high sets.

So, I think that there is a trend there. Obviously there are always exceptions, and some schools were genuinely seen to have policies where they were trying to put particular subject experts and great teachers with low sets. But for the most part, we see these trends where, whether it's that teachers are being actively rewarded and retained by being put with the top sets, or whether it's simply an assumption that the subject's experts should be going with the high set, that trend certainly seems to be playing out.

Do students notice if this happens?

The constant complaint from low-set students was that they were taught differently. And this was particularly noticeable where you had kids who might be in, say, a higher set for maths and a lower set for English, so were able to compare and contrast what they saw within their own experience.

And a continual theme exists of students feeling that they are being taught down to in low sets, that the curriculum was dumbed down for them, that they didn't have independent learning, that they weren't being pushed and challenged, and often there was the active use of the words "babying" and "babyish" among students.

So, there almost seemed to be an issue about feelings of respect and students feeling devalued. That's less about the quality of the teacher than the actual pedagogy and approach that's being deployed.

You talked before about best-practice setting. Is fluidity between the sets part of best practice and, if so, how is that done effectively?

It is part of best practice. If it's called attainment grouping, it needs to be about actual attainment. But there were a whole range of reasons that schools weren't able to do what we asked – things that we wouldn't have expected, [such as] the dominance of the timetable. I characterise this as the tail wagging the dog. Is this about the kids? Is this about learning? Or is it about some spreadsheet I call the timetable?

Does it fit the timetable puzzle, you mean? And, if not, the timetable wins?

Exactly. If you think about it, you can fit 30 in a class. If you have at the bottom of your attainment range, let's say, 10 kids with the same scores but you've only got five seats left in your class, you're going to have to decide. Five kids go into your top set and five go down to the middle, even though there's no difference in their prior attainment.

There's this mechanistic challenge which requires, inevitably, a teacher judgement for the kids on the margins. Which ones go into a top set, which go into the lower set? And surely that is where we would start to see bias coming into the system as well.

What impact do decisions like that have on how these kids view themselves?

Prior studies have shown that where you have kids with the same attainment levels, and some get placed in the higher attainment group and some get placed in a lower attainment group, the kids that get placed in the higher attainment group make better progress.

So, you can see that there is an impact there, presumably for a range of reasons. It might be the boost of self-confidence, it might be the high expectations or the quality of the teacher, and so forth, but that does have a positive impact.

They absolutely do get a sense of how the school views them. It does have an impact

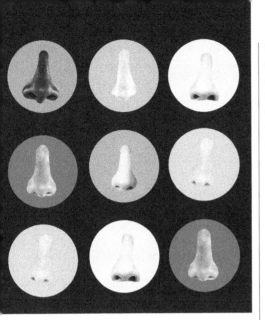

OK, so let's get back to mixed-attainment teaching: do we need to carefully consider grouping still in this model or can we run with the same mix of students that might be allocated to a tutor group? Do we need a quota of different attainment levels?

It's a really good question. In the mixed-attainment trial, we asked schools to make sure that each group reflected a proper balance and a range of different attainment backgrounds, and it may well be possible that there does need to be at least some care and potential tweaking to make sure that you do have a range of attainment. But we know about the challenges of transition, so things like friendship groups may be important – yet again, it's not clear-cut.

It seems a difficult topic to unpick...

It is a complex issue, and it may be that there are benefits and weaknesses to every approach we take to grouping students. What I'm trying to get to is the best, the most effective and the fairest practices, and particularly those that don't actively disadvantage kids from low socio-economic backgrounds, which we can see clearly is what's happening at the moment.

on their self-esteem and self-confidence, and again, this is something that our project has measured.

We found that there was a small but statistically significant correlation that students' self-confidence absolutely correlated with their set level.

We also know from the qualitative side of the work that students were often very frustrated or distressed by the set group that they'd been placed in. But I wouldn't want to suggest for a minute that this is true for every child or, indeed, that it's completely straightforward.

One of the things that's surprising to me, given the very strong messages children are receiving about their "ability", is the resilience of some children, who do not to seem to worry about that.

And, of course, there's good evidence in the prior literature that not all kids love being in a top set. Again, some might prefer to be thriving at the top of set two rather than struggling in the bottom of set one, and so on. It's not clear-cut.

This an edited transcript of a recorded interview that was published in February 2018. You can listen to the full interview here, bit.ly/BeckyFrancis

FURTHER READING

- Becky Francis on her latest EEF study, bit.ly/doubledisadvantage
- Sarah Wright on attainment grouping, bit.ly/30secondbriefing
- An EEF summary of the evidence about the effectiveness of setting and streaming, bit.ly/EEFsettingtoolkit

Chapter two

Dr Kathryn Asbury on the potential impact of genetics research

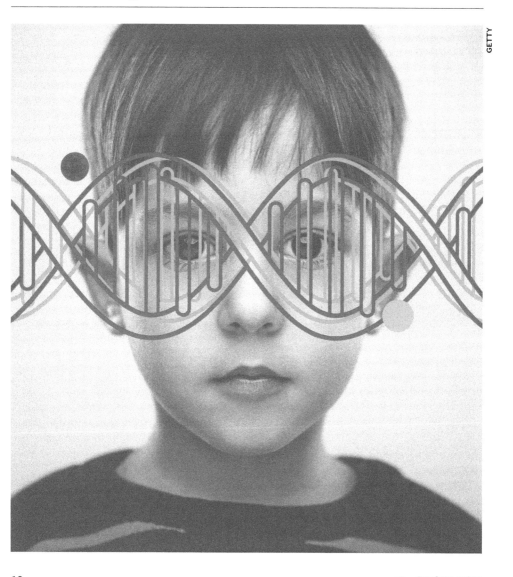

GETTY

Kathryn Asbury is a psychologist researching the implications of genetics for education at the University of York. She is also the author, with Robert Plomin, of *G is for Genes: The Impact of Genetics on Education and Achievement*. In this interview, she discusses why genetics research is so controversial and what teachers need to know about it.

Just the mention of the word genetics makes people nervous – spoken of in the context of education, it can make them even more wary. Why is that?
Genetics research has a difficult historical past that culminated in the Second World War, which, thankfully, brought the eugenics movement to an end. I think that genetics education research was tarnished by that.

People worry that if we take genetics into account when thinking about how human beings behave and, in particular, how children learn and develop, then that is going to lead to a situation in which we discriminate against the less able or those who are weaker or disadvantaged in society for any reason. So, I think the problem is not the research but the fears about how it might be used.

I do have sympathy for that and I think we have a duty to reassure people that this is not why we do this research: that is not the purpose of twin studies, or adoption studies, or behavioural genetic research in general.

You've been working on the twin study with Robert Plomin for well over a decade (the study itself began in 1994). In that time, have you seen any changes in how people perceive the research?
The twin study you mention is TEDS (www.teds.ac.uk) and, a few years ago,

there was a paper that looked at teacher views on the role of genetics in influencing how children learn. I have a PhD student doing something similar at the moment.

What we are finding is that teachers are actually really open to the ideas. When it is put objectively to them, they can see it makes sense; teachers accept that our genetic factors influence the behaviour that they see in the classroom. There is still this worry about actually using that information, though.

You have been very clear on numerous occasions, not least in the pages of *Tes*, that we do need to have this conversation about genetics in education; it's one that is necessary.
Yes, I think that is for two main reasons. The first is that everything is heritable. Everything a child is doing in a classroom – from learning to read, learning science, how they're playing with other children, how they're communicating with teachers, their mental health and wellbeing – is all influenced by their genes.

So, when something is such a central part of who children are and how they behave and, therefore, how we plan to meet their needs, it seems a bit bonkers not to talk about it. There's nothing else that we wouldn't include in the conversation if it was that central to what was actually happening. We've got this robust replicated and reliable research that has been around for decades and decades, it seems silly to ignore it and pretend that it's not there – we've got to talk about what it means.

The other reason is that there are developments in molecular genetic research at the moment. Scientists are increasingly finding genetic variants of a very tiny effect that are associated with aspects of learning and aspects of education. They're combining those genetic variants of tiny effect in what is known as genome-wide polygenic scores. The most recent score was EA3, released in summer 2018, which I looked at in a recent *Tes* article (bit.ly/DestinyAssistant).

I think what we will see is genome-wide polygenic scores that can explain a good chunk of the differences between children in aspects of their education and aspects of their learning.

It's really important to prepare for that. Some people are going to want to use this information: is that OK? Do we want to use it? How should we use it? How can we make it safe? How can we make sure that it is used for good purposes to benefit children in our schools?

I don't know how [the scores] will be used. That is a decision that society will take or individuals will take.

There are ethical, legal and regulatory issues that need to be seriously considered, otherwise we will be hit with a situation where a commercial company is using them and offering them to some people, and they're being used in ways that might be useful and might not.

So, I think we need to discuss, we need to prepare, but I'm not making predictions about when this will happen.

Is that similar to the Silicon Valley companies emerging now where you can send off a substantial amount of money and get your genome map back, or is this different?
It is different, so you can spit in a tube and send it off to a [genomics] company, such as 23andMe, and it will tell you your risk of things that range from liking asparagus right through to having Alzheimer's or curly hair – all sorts of things.

It will tell you whether your risk is slightly higher, lower or bang-on average. It's a probabilistic risk indicator rather than "this is what you're going to be like". That's all that research can ever offer; probabilistic risk. It's not deterministic in any way.

That is a common misconception about genetics, isn't it, that it is a sort of blueprint for your life? Do you want to talk about the common misconceptions? The main one, perhaps, is heritability...
Yes, I think that's a word that people commonly misunderstand and I think that it underpins some of the hostility that we do see towards genetic research.

People sometimes think that if we say that "shyness is 50 per cent heritable", what we're saying is that "how shy I am is 50 per cent explained by my genes", or "how shy you are is 50 per cent explained by your genes". Actually, this kind of research isn't talking about individuals at all: heritability is a population statistic; it's about individual differences.

So, if we take a large group of people and plot their shyness scores on a bell curve, then what heritability tells us is the extent to which those differences between people are explained by differences in their genes.

OK, so in terms of the miscommunication around the research, how much more could you do as an academic community to make that explicit? And how much of the education aspect needs to be something that other people address?
I see it as a really important part of my job, so when Plomin and I wrote *G is for Genes*, it was for that purpose. We wrote it for teachers and parents to try to explain what we know, what the research has shown.

GETTY

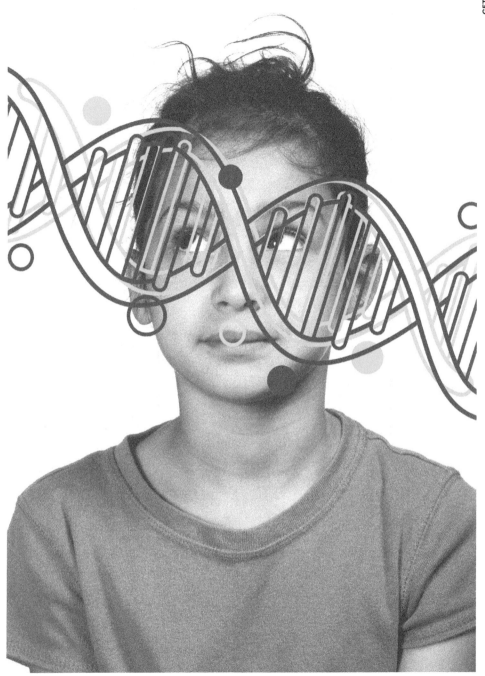

We take the opportunities that come our way to speak about genetics to non-academic audiences and, in particular, to teachers. But I'm sure that there is more that we can do. Whether that is through CPD, or information online, or more work in the media, I'm not sure, but I think we probably can do more.

Moving on to the research body itself, another thing you have mentioned in the past is how, whenever anyone talks about genetics in education, intelligence is the first port of call and, more often than not, the only one that anyone explores. You have stressed that there is a lot more we should consider.

All research, whether genetically informed or not, finds that cognitive ability is a really strong predictor of how children perform in school; possibly the strongest predictor.

But the research also finds that factors like motivation, self-efficacy, what is going on at home, the school environment and behaviour problems are all predictive of achievement as well.

And those things correlate with each other, so it's a very complex situation where you have got multiple behaviours interacting with each other and informing how well a child does at the end of the day.

So, some of my colleagues on the TEDS study looked at GCSE results in the UK a couple of years ago. They found that they had nine variables, including the ones that I mentioned, and they were all predictive of GCSE achievement.

And some of those links between the behaviour – whether that was self-efficacy or intelligence – and achievement, were caused by genetic influence as well. There were similar genetic factors influencing both things.

So, people can understand why intelligence might be genetically influenced, but might struggle with behaviour, motivation and self-efficacy. Why?

I'm not sure because, if you think about it from a parenting point of view, there's a commonplace saying that psychologists all believe in the priority of nurture until they have their second child. Then they think, "hang on, I treated them differently, but

GETTY

not that differently". Even looking at tiny babies, you can see evidence of different temperaments from the day they're born – actually much earlier than you're likely to see evidence of different cognitive abilities, which tend to show a bit later.

How fixed are these genetic influences?
US professor Eric Turkheimer came up with the laws of behavioural genetics and the first one is that everything is heritable. That seems to hold as a law.

What it means is a harder question because it certainly doesn't mean that you can't change something about yourself.

I'm 5ft 4in and height is one of our most heritable human characteristics, the heritability is close to 90 per cent. But I can wear heels, I can make myself appear taller, I can do things to change the effect of my genes and make myself different. We also know that vision is highly heritable but you can wear glasses and correct any effect of having poor vision.

One of the things we commonly say is that genetic influence is about what is but not about what can be.

What we know from a heritability estimate is that genetic factors matter. There are biological factors behind why some children find it harder to learn or to make friends or to read or do maths than others.

Maybe for that reason, for that biological reason, there are children who need extra help. We're very comfortable saying that, for social reasons, some children need extra help, for example, if they're eligible for free school meals or they have English as an additional language, or they've got a statement of special educational needs.

But would it be OK to say "for biological reasons, this child has a higher probability of finding reading difficult than other children: shall we go in with early interventions and extra support from the beginning?"

These are discussions that we need to have. If we have that information, how can we use it? Does it mean we go in at nursery, do we go in much earlier for children who have a high risk of experiencing difficulty? Is there a possibility that, at some point in the future, we can minimise the effect of difficulties to the extent that they don't really become difficulties in the classroom because we've addressed them already?

Common sense would say that the earlier the intervention, the better. Is that the case?

In the past, there was a belief that there was this neuroplastic period before children went to school in which, if you needed to change things, you needed to change it

then. Now we understand that development continues into early adulthood, so the window for intervention, change and making a difference is much wider than we thought it was.

That said, the pre-school years are, I think, probably the optimal time to intervene or to start that process of intervention for any child that is at risk of difficulty.

It depends on what that risk of difficulty is for. If the difficulty is with reading, it's very hard to access much of the curriculum [without being able to read] and so early intervention makes a great deal of sense there. Whereas there are other problems that are more likely to manifest around adolescence, maybe issues with mental health, and then intervention later is more appropriate there. I think you would need to take quite a nuanced approach depending on what you were trying to predict.

So, how far do teachers need to understand the science here, and how far is it just about teachers being aware of this strand of research and being unafraid of it?

What I would hope is that, by thinking about individual differences and understanding that such differences have a genetic basis, it could lead to more understanding educators, who are more sensitive and tolerant towards diversity in their classrooms.

Equally, I would have to admit that there is a risk – exactly the same as the free-school meals risk – that if you say this child is at risk of struggling or not achieving highly, you could reduce your expectations for that child. That would be equally wrong.

That's one of the things I think we need to assess and prepare for to make sure it doesn't pan out like that.

GETTY

This an edited transcript of a recorded interview that was published in February 2018. You can listen to the full interview here: bit.ly/Asburyongenetics

FURTHER READING

- See Kathryn Asbury's article about genetics and education, which appeared in *Tes* on 7 September 2018, bit.ly/DestinyAssistant
- The Twins Early Development Study, www.teds.ac.uk
- Emily Smith-Woolley on the latest genetics research into GCSE performance, bit.ly/GeneticsandGCSEs

Chapter three

Dr Jessie Ricketts on literacy support in secondary schools

GETTY

Jessie Ricketts leads the Learning and Reading Acquisition Laboratory at Royal Holloway, University of London. Her research focuses on the role of vocabulary in reading (word-level reading and comprehension) and, reciprocally, the role of reading in oral vocabulary acquisition. In this interview, she discusses literacy support in secondary schools.

Your recent research has looked at literacy support in secondary schools and how we teach reading in that phase, which is a strangely neglected topic in education discussions: so often, literacy is seen as having a primary focus...

Yes, I've been doing some work in secondary and the message is that we don't necessarily know what to recommend in terms of teaching reading at that stage because there is just so little research on reading in secondary.

Much of the focus seems to have been on vocabulary lists – teaching the key words to access a topic. What you have to be mindful of [with that approach] is that there is this set of words that you might want to teach [students] in order to be able to access the topic, but the descriptions you're using underneath those words also need to contain words that they're going to understand. You do have to remember that there are some children who arrive at secondary school with the kind of vocabulary knowledge that you would expect from a six-year-old.

It does become a very complex thing: trying to think about what the knowledge gaps might be in your class is tricky.

We were looking recently at some extracts from science textbooks. There was one on satellites and it struck me that you are very likely, in Years 7, 8, or 9, to have a child or many children who don't know what a satellite is, yet at no point in that textbook was it defined. It was just assumed that you would know what a satellite was. That wouldn't be true of all textbooks and texts, but it's important to be mindful of what those crucial words are and at least make sure that they're known.

There are those who will say that primary schools have failed their duty to that child if they have not learned these words?

It's a really tall order to expect every child to leave primary school with all of the knowledge and skills they need to enter secondary. My experience of teachers is that they're incredibly hard-working and they care a lot about what they do, and they're doing the very best that they can with the material, knowledge, time and resources that they have. So, it's unfortunate that, sometimes, people are forced into a situation where they feel that they need to do this blame game.

You've spoken before about children developing reading or comprehension issues later as well. Could it be that they've reached a plateau at Year 7 and, actually, they were doing fine at primary school but accessing the secondary curriculum is where the problem could first be identified?

That's really interesting that you say that and, certainly, we do see children who learn to read words quite well – so accurately and efficiently – and that's very much the focus of the curriculum early on in primary.

As they move through the system, though, sometimes you see those reading difficulties emerge, and they tend to be around language comprehension and reading comprehension. Sometimes we refer to those children as being poor comprehenders or children with specific reading difficulties.

So, yes, you can see reading difficulties that would impact on the curriculum, and access to the curriculum and exam performance, that emerge a little bit later.

What I would also say about this jump from primary to secondary is that the demands of the secondary setting are really quite different from the demands of the primary setting: the curriculum changes, of course, but also children are just expected to learn much more independently and they're also expected to be more independent. So, they're doing all sorts of things: finding their own way to all of these different classrooms throughout the day, managing a timetable in a very different way. In some ways, it can feel like a much less supportive environment.

On top of that, there are these added expectations in terms of what they will learn independently and how much homework they will do. That becomes increasingly part of how they will get their knowledge as they go up the secondary curriculum.

So, I think it's perfectly possible that there are children who were doing fine in primary school, who, on the move into secondary school, with all of these additional challenges, start to present with subtle difficulties that they were having in primary school but which have become much more pronounced [in secondary].

What have you found usually happens with these children?

I was increasingly visiting secondary schools and talking to teachers and special educational needs coordinators who were faced with this group of children, sometimes quite

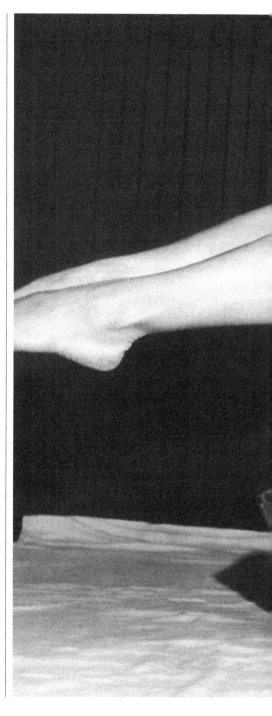

GETTY

a large group of children, who didn't really have functional reading abilities.

They didn't know what to do about it because, in the initial teacher education, or even in continuing professional development for secondary teachers, they don't get much information on the science of reading, what we know about how children learn to read, and what you might do in order to teach a child to read or to improve their reading skills. It's not really seen as the job of secondary teachers.

We need to have a shift in perception and realise that it would be a really good thing if, in every secondary school, we had at least one teacher who was skilled and had a good knowledge base in that topic, so that we can start to make sure that we are supporting those children at the bottom end of the distribution in secondary, because we know that they're there.

That's why I got interested in that line of research in the first place, really: trying to find out more about what the science of reading in adolescence looks like because, at the moment, we don't really know what's going on beyond the primary.

Often, I understand, secondary-age students are given primary resources or taught as if they are still in primary?
Yes, you do see in secondary schools that, because there are no alternative resources, teachers use things that are used regularly in primary schools. The children may well have [already] had these five years ago. They may be conscious of the fact that they were assigned for a much younger child.

I do think there could be much more work around trying to create age-appropriate resources for use in secondary and that this would make a big difference. A really interesting conversation I've been having quite

regularly with secondary school teachers at the moment is that, with poor readers, their primary concern may to some extent be the student's functional reading abilities and wanting to support that, but also they want to mitigate any issue in relation to motivation and attitude to learning.

Secondary teachers really do seem to feel that attitude to learning is the most important factor for success. If we can somehow harness that then we would be able to get kids into a better place.

Can children hide their difficulties?
What we know from the work that we've done with primary-aged children is that reading comprehension difficulties really can be quite hidden.

It is very difficult to detect such difficulties, even in the primary setting, where there is this real focus on literacy.

If anything, that's probably likely to be compounded by the time we get to secondary school, where it may even be very difficult to detect word-reading difficulties. By that point, you can imagine that children may well have developed all sorts of strategies to cover up for that fact that they're not reading and not understanding what they're reading. It does become very difficult.

Is there anything you would recommend in these situations?
In order to do a reliable reading comprehension assessment with a child, you really want to be doing it one on one.

And what about general things that could be done at a system level to help support literacy in secondary?
We need to have some kind of system in place that "upskills" secondary teachers and

secondary schools generally. Give them the knowledge and resources that they need to support these pupils. We really need to shine a light on secondary and be supporting what's happening there.

This an edited transcript of a recorded interview that was published in February 2018. You can listen to the full interview here, bit.ly/Oralvocab_iskey

FURTHER READING

- *Tes* talks to Jessie Ricketts about the importance of oral language in reading, bit.ly/Testalks_Ricketts
- Researchers find a more balanced approach to competing theories on teaching reading, bit.ly/Readingwars_ceasefire
- Why wordlists don't work, bit.ly/Dictionary_hard

Chapter four

Rob Webster on effective deployment of teaching assistants

Rob Webster is a senior researcher at the Centre for Inclusive Education, UCL Institute of Education. From 2011-17, he led two research projects (Making a Statement and SEN in Secondary Education) which, together, make up the UK's largest observational study of the educational experiences of pupils with special educational needs and disability (SEND). He was involved in the groundbreaking Deployment and Impact of Support Staff (DISS) project and now leads the Maximising the Impact of Teaching Assistants initiative, which is also the focus of a large-scale trial, funded by the Education Endowment Foundation (EEF). In this interview, he discusses effective deployment of teaching assistants.

Shall we start by looking at the first big TA research study you were involved in, DISS? It made many headlines...

There was a team of six and a slightly extended group of people who spent five years on that study. It was a huge bit of work and there isn't anything like it that has been done before or since, anywhere in the world, as far as we know.

When it came out, it turned on its head the commonsense logic that if you give children who are struggling the most adult support, that's got to be a good thing for them. The project showed that TAs were actually having a negative impact academically compared with those that weren't having that support from TAs, or very little by comparison.

What about a pupil's motivation, their levels of confidence, their independence and so on?

We didn't find anything consistent in that at all. We were very careful when the study came out – we wanted to be really clear in our messaging that TAs weren't and aren't to blame. They're not the problem here – in a sense, they're being caught in the crossfire. It's entirely about the decisions that are made about how they're used, across the school and school leadership, and across the classroom as well.

But there were a few headlines and reactions along the lines of "the research says that TAs are useless"...

This comes up every so often and I get challenged with, "your research said that TAs are useless and we should get rid of them". I've never said that, and never get tired of saying that I never said that. It really matters as well, because if people run away with the idea that teaching assistants are somehow the problem, and that idea gets some political traction – as it seemed to a few years ago – then the implications are really quite serious.

GETTY

So, the research was really about poor utilisation of TAs rather than that the role was not needed?

Yes, there is a body of research we don't talk enough about, and that is what happens when you have TAs delivering structured intervention programmes – the kind of things that arrive off the shelf. Schools use them all of the time and TAs can be trained to deliver them. The outcomes there, the general message from that research, is profoundly positive.

You only have to look at the seven or so studies that the EEF funded in the past few years to see that. Each is showing positive effects of between two and four months. This is quite unheralded. You don't often see research like this line up so consistently, and it leaves us with a clear view that this is a good example of what we mean when we speak to schools about how best to use TAs.

We should be using them to supplement the teaching, not replace teachers; to deliver structured intervention programmes to supplement what is going on in the classroom, and then you capitalise on that in terms of the wider learning and test scores.

Could that be for the high attainers as well as the low attainers?

There's no reason why not. That could free up the teacher to be working with the children who are struggling most – as long as TAs are well-trained, well-supported, they are given the resources and time to do the job, and the timetabling is secure.

Would you say the role of TA has become more professional?

The standard has risen. We come across schools where it is a graduate-only job now. There's no standard entry. There have, over time, been attempts to try to standardise

that, but they never took off. There's something to be said for having some kind of training because that's patchy. TAs don't consistently get CPD or induction.

Is that an attitude problem – are they still seen almost as parent volunteers? Or is it a finance issue, or a combination of the two?

I'm sure that the financing plays an issue, but then, going back some years when money wasn't so much of an issue, we didn't

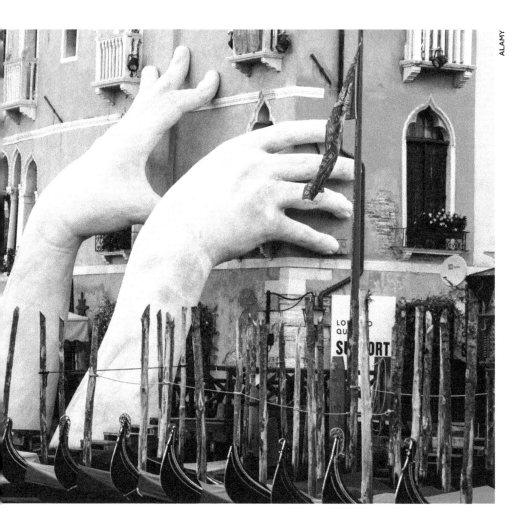
ALAMY

have training then, either. What was the thinking behind that? Would they just come in and learn on the job? Maybe there was a sense that "this is a role that you can learn on the job – how hard can it be to look after kids who are struggling with the basics?".

You only need to think about that for a few seconds longer to know that it is quite challenging. To look after children who are struggling with the basic concepts – these are instructional challenges, there are pedagogic issues here that some teachers would struggle with, and we're asking people to come in cold off the street, who maybe don't have a graduate qualification to do it. You can then start to see why we found what we found in the DISS project.

Is there a better understanding and greater appreciation of the role among classroom teachers compared with leadership teams?

When we work with schools in our programmes and our projects, we very purposefully direct the first phase of it at school leaders, because we know that they're the ones who have got their hands on the levers to make the most change.

Does the problem go higher than them, even, to a policy level?

One of the policy black holes that we've had from the very start was that we've never really decided what we want TAs to do. And we've not decided what we don't want them to do. We've said to schools, "you work it out". We've used the autonomy card to say "you have the freedom to decide, it's your resource you do with it as you wish".

So, what's going to happen? You're going to have very variable practices, even within the same school, let alone across schools. There's no standard way of using TAs.

In some schools, it's fine that TAs can take cover for a whole day. In other schools, they say "we don't think that's appropriate, we get a supply teacher in".

And then there is the whole notion of support. You talk to teachers, headteachers and Sendcos about what TAs do, and they will tell you that they support teachers with statements and planning, they support the lower attainers, they support the teacher, the teaching, the curriculum and they support the learning.

But those conceptualisations of support get quite fuzzy. What does it look like? How do I know really good support from support that is well-meaning but is leading to that learned helplessness?

So, poor use of TAs can become child-minding rather than teaching?

Yes, at its worst. For example, you can get stereo teaching, which is where the teacher will be doing their whole-class delivery and the TA, while very well-meaning, will be repeating what the teacher is saying to one or two kids at the side of the classroom. It's like a satellite delay effect that is going on in the room.

That might be off-putting for the teacher but you bring it back to the child and say "what's their experience of this, then?" They're toggling between two adult voices, which could be quite difficult.

It comes from a well-meaning place; there's not a criticism of TAs here. We haven't, as a school or a system, pinned down what we think makes good support, or said what we think that we ought to be avoiding and why. So, we get a drift towards doing what looks most helpful.

What does effective deployment look like – you mentioned the idea of trained TAs running interventions earlier, but what else?

We have to start with the pupils. If that is our starting point, then we might look at some of the challenges we have.

One example might be the lesson cover thing – TAs getting pulled off the corridor to cover lessons.

That has a knock-on effect on other things that they might have been doing. They're conflicted because they can't say no, so they go and do it.

Is there a case in a school, for example, of having one or two TAs whose job it is to do lesson covers? We've had cover supervisors for a little while in secondary school, but that job didn't really fit the primary model.

Maybe now there is a case for looking at that. For a cover lesson, the inconvenience is built in – you're expected to be disrupted and you have one or two TAs who can cover that.

GETTY

That means the TAs whose job it is to do intervention programmes can crack on and do that uninterrupted.

Maybe, rather than lots of TAs doing lots of different interventions, you have an elite squad. They do the interventions; they're the experts.

They have the experience, they can build that expertise?

Exactly. Then we look back inside the classroom – there may be some call for a more administrative role. Maybe from the teacher workload point of view, the well-being point of view, having someone who can do some of the admin will be really useful for the teachers and perhaps TAs are happy to do that.

Then you've got the classroom group and we really need to think very hard about how we're using that resource in the classroom, and how the teachers are using those TAs to supplement and not replace them.

It has to be a different way than [the teacher saying to the TA], "I'm going to teach these 25, you take those five. Here's the lesson plan. Good luck. Tell me how the lesson went". It needs to be a lot more strategic than that.

The teachers should be thinking about where they need to be, how they place the TA in relation to where they are: "You walk around the classroom, make sure everyone is on task for five minutes, while I deal with these two or three kids that clearly need additional input".

So, it is not just about leaders tapping into the research – a change of attitude is needed among teachers, too?

There is a responsibility and accountability issue here. If you're a teacher, you're responsible for the learning of all of the children in your class, so if you are sending some of them out, you are getting more disconnected from their learning.

They're doing intervention programmes and you don't know how they're doing. You're not capitalising on the learning that could kick them on in their wider targets.

This an edited transcript of a recorded interview that was published in March 2018. You can listen to the full interview here, bit.ly/UseTAswisely

FURTHER READING
- How to make the most of your TAs, maximisingtas.co.uk
- Rob Webster on the myth of inclusion, bit.ly/inclusionmyth
- Six steps to effective TA interventions, bit.ly/TAinterventions

Chapter five

Dr Christian Bokhove
on how to read research

Christian Bokhove is associate professor in mathematics education within the Southampton Education School at the University of Southampton. He was a teacher of mathematics and computer science and head of ICT at a secondary school in Zaandam, the Netherlands, from 1998 to 2012. Here, he talks about the difficulties teachers experience using and applying research.

The world of academic research can often seem impenetrable because of the language used and the complexity of the methodologies. Do teachers really have the time or training to make sense of that world?

It is a difficult process. One reason I'm on social media is that you have the wisdom of the crowds helping you, sending you interesting papers and findings. But, of course, in that process of translating complex papers and findings into soundbites – 280 character soundbites, now – that is difficult, as well.

So, you do need to be careful that you don't get Chinese whispers, almost, where you start off with a very complex situation and basically you morph this nuanced message of an academic into 280 characters that sometimes feels like a good representation but, just as often, seems like a bit of a shortcut.

Is that process of trying to simplify a research message often done in an ideological way, or is it a simple misunderstanding, or a lack of time to fully appreciate the argument or, perhaps, a mix of all three?

All the above, I think. One interesting thing to look at is pairs of psychological terms where there is confusion as, in daily life, you would simply use them interchangeably. For example, the word "significant" in statistics has a specific meaning, but "significant" in the phrase "something significant happened in my life", that has a sort of daily meaning as well.

Similarly, the word "reliability". Would you buy a car from someone who is unreliable? Of course not. Who would buy a car from an unreliable person?

But "reliability" also has a specific research methods connotation and there are different types of reliability. If, for example, we mark [an exam] paper and you do this and I do this, and then we look where we have marked it in the same way and we get the same score, then we have reliability.

However, the word can also be about test/retest reliability. So, if I give one test to a student on day one and, 10 days later, I give the same test, will the score be exactly the same? That's a different type of reliability.

We use labelling often, of course, to summarise, in one word, what we mean. But it does make sense to sometimes probe a little deeper whether we really have a common understanding of the term that we are talking about.

You have talked in the past about publication bias – the unseen research that might skew our view, if we could see it...

I would say publication bias might be one of the biggest challenges for academia or science in general because, perhaps, it's quite human that you want something special to arise from a piece of research.

However, it's actually not very realistic to expect that because a lot of things don't work. The problem is, we don't know up front what will work and what won't, so that means it's quite reasonable to expect a

ALAMY

lot of so-called "no" results, where there is no effect or nothing has happened, and nothing comes out of it.

But when you want to go and publish in journals – especially, some would say, the bigger, more prominent ones – then it would be difficult to get into those journals if your result is, "yeah, nothing special really happened". And I think we all understand why that is, but it poses a big problem because it means that, in those journals, you basically get the positive results, the favourable results.

And those are the journal articles that we then use to present a certain case to say, "oh, look, in meta-analysis, 100 studies said that it would work, so it must really be working because otherwise there wouldn't have been 100".

But that is only because those 100 have been published, and what is almost impossible to find out is how many studies have there been that have never been published and just ended up in a big drawer? And because it's notoriously hard to find out, it's very hard to tackle it.

That's obviously just one consideration when looking at research. There's so much more, isn't there? Does it take a lot of time to fully interrogate a research paper?
A lot of time, if you really do close reading. If you want to dive into, for example, the instruments or the wording of the questions or even the statistical methods, or checking citations, you're talking about hours, realistically.

And that's for someone like you, who knows what they're looking for, essentially?
Yes.

That seems a big ask of teachers who have limited time. Should they be trying to get a grip on an area by trawling a single study?
I would say refrain from big conclusions until you have a fuller overview of the situation. In that sense, meta-reviews try to do exactly that, but you can't completely rule out that there might still be some kind of bias, for example, in what studies you include. Some people would say, "everything qualitative, away with it – not rigorous enough", which I think would be a shame because [qualitative studies] often give a richer picture of the situation, but it is harder to generalise from them.

So, I would say that I think it's useful to analyse an article and read articles, but perhaps more to get a sense of the enormous complexity and variables that are at play rather than [expecting] a silver bullet at the end. You could argue that, because science is incremental, we build on previous science and we keep on building – one study will never be enough; it's actually the whole body of knowledge that builds.

It sounds like what we should be building is a very nuanced picture of any research area, not looking for simple answers that do not exist?
I think so. I like the word "nuance". There is a task in the master's qualification we run where we ask students to study a wall. A lot of students think, "what are you talking about, a wall?" But you can actually record a lot of things about the wall, such as the temperature. You can look at the construction: what is it made of? Where is it standing? Is it part of a larger structure? Over time, what happened with the wall?

We just study the wall and we look at scientific parts, but then there's also the

more interpretive part and the history. Students find it incredibly difficult, and never realise how many things you can actually study from something so mundane as a wall.

Then we make the link to humans because a wall is static and it doesn't have thought, and humans do. Replace [this idea of] the wall with one human and then [students] realise immediately that it becomes infinitely more complex. Then [replace it with] several humans who can communicate and it becomes even more complex.

It is complex, so why pretend otherwise? I understand why, because it sometimes makes things more bearable; our life and discussions easier.

So, do you think teachers need to be more aware of this and academics need to be more explicit about it?
Absolutely. That is the way forward. I think you need this cooperation. We can say it is great if they would work together

more but the infrastructure needs to be in place to actually do this. In this call for evidence-informed practice, [cooperation] doesn't seem to be something that is very high on the agenda. The theme is high on the agenda, but really helping to sort the barriers for actually doing this? I don't get the feeling that is being serviced. It would be great if it was.

This an edited transcript of a recorded interview that was published in January 2018. You can listen to the full interview here, bit.ly/Research_oversimplification

FURTHER READING
- Dylan Wiliam on the nine things every teacher should know, bit.ly/Wiliam9things
- Nick Rose on the seven pillars of classroom practice, bit.ly/Rose_7pillars
- Tes talks to Steve Higgins, bit.ly/Talks_Higgins

Chapter six

Professor Kalwant Bhopal
on racism in education

GETTY

K alwant Bhopal is professor of education and social justice, professorial research fellow and deputy director of the Centre for Research in Race and Education in the School of Education, University of Birmingham. Her research focuses on the achievements and experiences of minority ethnic groups in education, which is the topic of the following discussion.

Many would claim racism has been largely banished from education – your research suggests otherwise?

We've had significant advances in policy-making: such as, the introduction of the Equality Act and the widening participation agenda. We also have an increase in the number of black, Asian and minority ethnic (BAME) students in higher education (I must note there are differences within and between that term of BAME and I'm aware of the problematics. However, I will use it for ease of conversation in this discussion).

But despite significant advances, inequalities persist. In my research, I argue that this is for various reasons. First, we have processes of marginalisation and exclusion, which contribute to institutional racism within the education system.

Second, we have a lack of representation of BAME individuals in decision-making roles. Third, we don't have a curriculum that's diverse and, fourth, we have a system that continues to maintain "whiteness" and white privilege in the perpetuation of who is successful and who is not.

By the curriculum, do you mean the language of the curriculum or its content that's problematic?

It's both. One of the questions I often get asked is about diversifying the curriculum

in higher education, but we have to move further back.

We have to start at primary-school level and through secondary school, and think about, for instance, how history is taught to our young children, and about how the diversity of our historical experience is hugely important, so that young people are growing up with a diverse understanding of our historical experience in the UK rather than its being focused on one single Eurocentric model.

Do you think when teachers make curriculum choices, there's an unconscious racism at work that is perpetuated by the structures they work within?

That's a very difficult question because I think that there are two things there. First, it quite often depends on the leadership team in a particular school.

So, for example, if you have a leader who is very interested in a diverse curriculum and wants to look at the way in which diversity is displayed, then that will be pushed from that end. Second, I think teachers are under a lot of pressure to make sure that they are teaching particular things that need to be taught in terms of the curriculum itself. I like to think that it isn't a conscious thing that's done.

It's something that teachers need to be aware of, in the sense that they need to understand that diversity benefits everyone. Diversity benefits students, it benefits teachers and it benefits the whole community and society.

Let's not forget, at the same time, there are social structures and institutional racism that take place at all levels. I'm not saying that's an individual issue; I think we have to start dismantling and disrupting the social structures that continue to perpetuate the notion of whiteness.

That brings us to another of your four points: the marginalisation and exclusion of BAME students. You can see that clearly in the exclusion stats: if you're a black male, you're much more likely to be excluded from school. Why do you think that statistic exists? Is it a poor understanding of the individuals, the community? Is it an indication that teachers are targeting this group of students? Is it a curriculum issue?

That's an interesting and important question. The figures do suggest that if you're a black male, you're more likely to be excluded. If you're black, you're less likely to leave university with a 2.1 or a first. You're more likely to be unemployed six months after graduation, for instance. A number of things contribute to this.

Within the school system itself, it's important to look at the reasons why these young boys are being excluded. There has been a long history of stereotypes existing around young black boys and what that means in terms of masculinity and violence.

Those stereotypes continue to exist in all areas of life and there's a perpetuation of this being the case, whereas, in fact – if you look at some of the qualitative research – there's a lot of evidence to suggest that these young boys want to go to school and want to be successful.

In many cases, it's the system that is holding them back and this is perpetuated by institutional racism.

Is this an area in which teachers need more training?

Oh, absolutely. In a piece of research that we carried out about five years ago, where we interviewed trained teachers, they said that they only received one session on race and racism, and how to deal with it. So, many of our teachers are not equipped; they don't have the training in terms of knowing how to deal with racism or racist incidents if they actually take place within the classroom, and that is hugely important.

What's also important is that we need more black and minority ethnic individuals in senior decision-making roles in schools. Headteachers tend to be white and male, teachers tend to be white and female. That's what the overall statistics tell us, so if you're a child in a school and you're being taught a curriculum that's not very diverse, by someone who doesn't look like you, you're less likely to be motivated and want to be a teacher and go into that role.

Are some schools getting this right?

Some schools are better at it than others. It often depends on the area in which the school is located, but especially in this current economic, political and social climate, which is very troubled, given some of the political issues that are going on in the world, it's really important for us to be explicit about issues around race and racism.

In the classroom, we need to tell students – and we need teachers to understand it, too – that we are living in this climate where racism is considered to be OK in some respects, because of the political issues that have gone on.

But we have to teach individuals that diversity is a good thing and that acceptance is a good thing, because if we don't do that in the classroom, we're lost.

It's really difficult to understand how to make those changes in relation to how racism is understood because there's also a faction of society that feels that we've dealt with racism, let's move on. But post-racism is a myth. Racism continues at all levels of society and it starts at the school level.

Does a lot of the change have to come at a system, not classroom level, though?

Yes. Individual schools should have institutional frameworks that facilitate change and they should be made to address what those outcomes are on a practical level.

What are they going to do to increase the number of BAME students or staff in senior decision-making roles? Also, [there needs to be] a recognition and valuing of diversity in the curriculum and staff make-up.

We need some kind of institutional change...a governmental initiative that looks at reviewing staff profiles to identify under- and over-representation of individuals at particular levels, positions and types of contracts that they're on. Finally, we need to acknowledge and address institutional racism, because a failure to acknowledge results is a failure to act. If you acknowledge institutional racism and you acknowledge white privilege, then you can address it.

Are you hopeful for the future?

We've gone backwards instead of forwards. In my latest book, I present specifics and evidence to suggest that racism is alive in terms of looking at education, wealth, poverty, who has the highest jobs, health, etc – I look at all different areas.

But I am hopeful, I am optimistic, because even though we live in troubled times globally, the future generations give me hope. Younger generations are far more accepting and far more inclusive about diversity at all levels – not just race but also sexuality, gender, age, disability.

I am optimistic; these young people are our future and, if they have these attitudes of inclusion now, our hope is that we will live in a society that does value social justice and equity for all groups.

This an edited transcript of a recorded interview that was published in January 2018. You can listen to the full interview here, bit.ly/Bhophalonracism

FURTHER READING

- *Tes* talks to University of Birmingham academic David Gillborn, bit.ly/Testalk_Gillborn
- Headteacher Angela Browne on diversity in the teaching profession, bit.ly/Browneondiversity
- Leadership careers advice for BAME teachers, bit.ly/Diversityinleadership

Chapter seven

Professor Daniel Muijs on evaluating teacher and school effectiveness

GETTY

Daniel Muijs is head of research at Ofsted. He was formerly professor of education at the University of Southampton and associate dean, research and enterprise, in the Faculty of Social, Human and Mathematical Sciences. He also previously worked as professor of pedagogy and teacher development at the University of Manchester, professor of school leadership and management at the University of Newcastle, and as senior lecturer in quantitative research methods at Warwick Institute of Education. In this interview, he discusses teacher and school evaluation.

If you were a headteacher looking to evaluate how staff were performing, what does the research suggest you should do in that situation?

What it suggests is that you need a relatively holistic approach. So, you should not rely on any one individual method, be it observation, student attainment results or what people say about the individual. There is no one method that is going to give you a reliable view of that, so if you are looking within school to evaluate, then it's best to base it on a range of different sources and different data to try to inform that judgement. We find that the more holistically you look at that, the more likely you are to get to a valid end point.

Yet so much of how a teacher is viewed seems still to be tied to the results of their pupils...

You could never attribute the attainment of pupils purely to what the teacher does. The biggest predictor of students' attainment is their own prior attainment. So, if you have a particularly weak cohort in the year, it would be entirely unfair to judge a teacher, or indeed a school, just on that one year's data.

You need to look at that over a period so that those kind of cohort effects get ironed out. Or you need to do some kind of value-added measurement so that you're taking into account the starting point of the pupil and not just the end point.

With a progress measure, I guess?

Yes, absolutely. Though, of course, you have to be careful with that as well, especially when you are looking at individual teachers, because your cohort size is, by definition, quite small if you're looking at one particular classroom.

What you then have is a very large confidence interval, so your value-added estimates are not particularly reliable. Again, I would not advocate judging teacher performance based on value-added measures alone.

What about pedagogy – can a school leader judge how effective certain teaching methods are?

It's dangerous to say that there is one particular method that is always going to work in any classroom, in any school. Teaching is a partly contextual activity, so it's about the interaction between the teacher, the students and the curriculum of the particular subject that will determine what works and what doesn't.

Of course, teachers have different skill sets as well, so it would be dangerous to judge [based] on just one teacher in a school as being the practice that everybody then should be doing.

That doesn't mean to say that there shouldn't be any consistency in what happens in a school, though, because we do know that pupils benefit from a feeling of consistency and coherence in terms of what happens in a particular school environment.

Consistency of approach is really what I'm talking about in that respect. So, I would say that the evidence on how stringent you need to be on, for example, behaviour is not that clear yet. But what we do know is that consistency of approach within a school – a shared vision on what that is, a shared approach for teachers as well – is important. What pupils find frustrating is if they can do X with Teacher A and they can't do that with Teacher B. That's something that really gets their backs up and that causes problems in the school.

How about school evaluation, then? Can we easily compare schools?

Context matters. And we know that it matters. And we know that, say, Southampton is not London, so some of the issues are different.

However, it's going too far to say that things are so different that there's nothing we can possibly learn from the school down the road. When you look at a lot of the practices that you see in schools that are particularly effective, they are actually quite similar. So, we need to find a balance between what are, again, the more generic elements and what are the contextual elements within school effectiveness. And they are both important. Yes, we can learn, but we have to be careful that we take context into account.

Sometimes connecting schools in different parts of the country can be very valuable because it can be the case that, actually, your context is more similar to a school in Devon than it is to the school nearest to you in Norfolk.

What can also be an advantage in that respect is that the school in Devon is not

really your competitor, so it can sometimes be easier to talk with a school that is further away from you. That is a very helpful thing that we can try to improve these systems.

So, in assessing schools, then, context is important, but how do we also get over our own bias, be it in a peer evaluation or Ofsted inspectors going into a school?

That is, of course, difficult because we are all influenced by the context in which we

GETTY

work. Here's an area where knowing some of the research can be helpful because that will point you to different models that also work and to some differences in context that may not be immediately obvious.

Disadvantaged areas are not all the same. They are disadvantaged in different ways. And there is more than one way to skin a cat in terms of making a school effective.

So, the first thing to do is be aware of different models that exist and different

models that work. Also, the more schools you visit, the more you become aware of differences in context.

There are so many variables involved in evaluating a school or individual teacher. In the research, how is that tackled? How do they isolate the variables?

The the first thing is, obviously, a school's not a laboratory, so we can't do a purely experimental approach where we say,

"OK, this is the variability we're going to use; let's randomly assign pupils".

Inevitably, what you are going to have to do is take into account as many of the different variables that may affect what you're looking at as possible, which is one of the reasons why educational research is quite complex, because you tend to have to look at quite a lot of different things.

You can't just isolate the particular things a teacher does. You need to collect data on the pupils or even contextual data. You need some data on school policies because, of course, a teacher does not work in isolation; the list can go on. And that is why we end up with these quite difficult studies.

Teaching is a science and an art, and there is an element of expertise to it that is not necessarily captured in research evidence. So, it's never the case that you can just take a research approach and apply it. It's also about the expertise of the teacher as a professional, who goes in there with knowledge of the individual kids, with knowledge of what's worked before in the school – it's always a mixture of those things.

Where do you think we need more research around schools, and school and pupil evaluation?

There are still so many areas that need research, so it's hard to pin down a particular area. There are still questions about how you translate some of those things from research into class in practice.

We are, in some ways, in a fortunate position in education, that there is a lot of work for us still to do.

This an edited transcript of a recorded interview that was published in March 2018. You can listen to the full interview here, bit.ly/Daniel_Muijs

FURTHER READING
- Nick Rose on finding success in failure, bit.ly/SuccessinFailure
- Improving the accuracy of lesson observations, bit.ly/Flawed_observations
- Liz Robinson on the importance of teacher self-evaluation, bit.ly/teacher_self-assessment

Tes RESEARCH

Chapter eight

Professor Vanita Sundaram on gender and 'lad culture' in schools

ALAMY

V anita Sundaram is professor of education at the University of York. Her research has focused on sexual harassment and gender-based violence in education settings; the development of research-informed prevention models; methodologies for conducting research on harassment and violence with children and young people; and the content and role of sex and relationships education. In this interview, she discusses gendered behaviour specifically related to sexual harassment, coercion and violence, and around "lad culture" and what schools can do to tackle it.

Do you want to start by outlining the research you've done in schools around these topics?

It has mainly involved secondary-age pupils and that's been focused mainly on their understanding of what violence is; so what constitutes violence, and building on a vast body of feminist research that exists on the fact that young people accept and tolerate violence.

That research has really shown that young people's understanding of violence is not lacking in any way, so school initiatives that would seek to try to point out to young people what violence is would miss the aim. Young people do know what violence is; they can recognise a range of forms of violent behaviour.

What's interesting, though, is the fact that they initially say that violence is unacceptable, so if you ask them what they think about violence, they'll always start off by saying "it's wrong", "you shouldn't do it", "it's naughty" and phrases like that.

But as you begin to talk about different scenarios in which coercive control, or harassment, or pressure or abuse might happen, they begin to justify why violence might

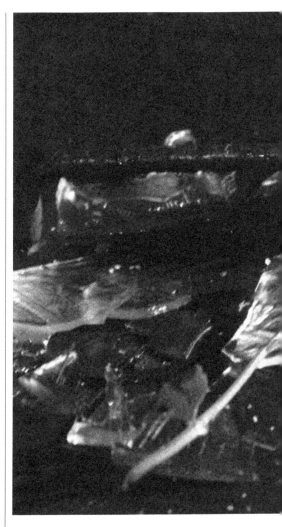

take place, and they do that with reference to gendered expectations and stereotypes.

So, if I was to break that down, I could give a couple of scenarios where a young man might be putting sexual pressure on his girlfriend at a party or in a social situation, and then the girlfriend says "no" and he continues to pressure her, and pushes her and calls her a gendered insult, such as "slut" or something like that.

will go along and be sexually acquiescent, and so, therefore, the violence might be deserved [if they don't comply].

That's quite shocking...
Well, they've got these very essentialist ideas of what boys and girls are like, or what men and women are like, and they're very biologically based. They talk about the nature of men and how they can't help themselves but be violent.

And then they talk a lot about the roles of girls in relationships and the fact that girls should be passive, they should be submissive, they should listen to their boyfriends, they should do what they ask them to do, including in relation to sex. And so, even though they think violence is wrong, they end up excusing it.

Where do those attitudes come from?
That's a tricky question to answer, but I think what we mustn't do is blame young people themselves. What I wouldn't want to do is take an individualised approach to this and say individual children who don't understand that violence is wrong are somehow deficient or lacking or naughty or bad. Really, we can't divorce their views on gender and violence from the wider social and cultural context in which they live, in which they're socialised.

So, we know from a very young age, we can really see how gendered norms are learned and enacted in primary schools.

Boys are using objectifying language about girls to evaluate their appearance, girls use that same language to talk about themselves and to evaluate their peers.

They're starting to absorb and learn how to be boys and how to be girls in very particular ways, and that is directly linked to their understandings, then, of when

What we find is that young people rely on gendered expectations or stereotypes about how they think boys should behave and how they think girls should behave, or what girls should put up with, to justify and explain– and sometimes excuse – violence.

They'll say things like, "oh, it's understandable because she rejected him sexually and boys don't like that kind of thing", or there's an expectation that girls violence is acceptable or not and what behaviours in general are acceptable or not.

Are there messages in schools that are facilitating those gendered roles?

Few schools consider themselves to be promoting particular gendered norms or ideas about sexuality. But schools do promote lessons about boys and girls – and heterosexuality, in particular – all the time.

Teachers do that through anecdotes about their relationships, their personal lives, they do it by talking about straight relationships in the media – for example, the royal wedding. So without necessarily explicitly realising it, they are normalising heterosexuality and making homosexuality unspeakable or positioning it as a threat to children's knowledge about sex and gender.

Also, teachers use gendered language all the time in schools, and that's one thing, if we are going to think about initial teacher education around these issues, we really need to recognise: the ways in which teachers are gendered beings in themselves, and the ways in which they have absorbed beliefs and enact beliefs about gender when they're interacting with children and young people. [I'm talking about] language like "boys and girls", that arbitrary division of classroom spaces, school spaces, into these binary categories of boys and girls, and the kind of stereotypes that go with that.

Those kinds of things absolutely reinforce in children's and young people's minds this notion that there are two genders, and that boys behave in a particular way and girls behave in another.

Is it a complicating factor that the profession is three-quarters female?

It's a complicated debate. There are many good reasons to diversify teaching as a profession but, unfortunately, a lot of the debates that have been put forward around why we need more male teachers have drawn on very essentialist notions of gender, so men can promote a particular type of masculinity in boys or they can speak better to boys. Those ideas of gender are really unhelpful to moving us forward in the debate.

There's been some research with male teachers who talk about schools feeling like feminised spaces but, again, pinpointing exactly what that is and why it's exclusionary to men is not so easy to establish.

It is common in schools to talk about the gap between the attainment of boys and girls, or gendered splits in subjects – is that helpful?

Thinking about nursery and early-years settings, we can already see that staff working in those situations come with their own beliefs about gender.

They will say that boys don't like to write, they don't like to sit still, they like to be outside and they like to be learning kinesthetically, whereas girls like to sit still.

So, are we exposing children to a particular set of opportunities and skills at a very early age and then, later on, talking about those as their natural qualities?

We've arrived at a point where it's very tempting to talk about these things as natural attributes of boys and girls because we can see patterns of similarity across societies as well.

Is it about a school culture then, or do we need to explicitly teach about gender in schools?

It's the job of schools to teach young people about structural and systemic inequality. We still live in a deeply racist society, we still live in a deeply sexist society, we still live in a deeply homophobic society, and to reduce that down to the level of the individual – and an individual's choices and negotiations of society – is very dangerous and damaging to those individuals who are on the receiving end of discrimination or disadvantage because of those inequalities.

So, I think it is the job of schools to raise young people's awareness around that while thinking about how we empower young people to challenge these inequalities and negotiate their lived experiences within that context.

Do teachers need a lot more training for that? Do you think that's an initial teacher-training problem? Do you think that means we need specialist teachers for that purpose?
There are lots of things that teacher education doesn't currently encompass, and I understand the pressures on teacher educators to fit it all in. So, it's not a criticism but I think we could do better.

What often gets left out of this discussion is that teaching has an emotional base and there's some really interesting research that's been done about the discomfort teachers feel around teaching about sexuality, for example.

Fundamentally, teacher education needs to enable teachers to recognise their own discomforts around gender, sexuality, sex, race, culture, language, religion and so on. Because we all bring our own values into the classroom – and teachers certainly do.

In relation to whether it should be a specialist teacher, it should be a well-trained teacher. I don't know whether that should be a sort of specialist.

I'm probably of the view that all teachers should be able to respond to racism, sexism and homophobia. And all teachers should be aware of their own racism, sexism and homophobia in order to challenge that when they see it in their school context. But that might be an unrealistic aim, so it might be that the resources have to be invested in specialist staff in schools.

But I certainly think senior management should be well-trained, so they should always have the specialism in relation to being able to deal with these issues.

This an edited transcript of a recorded interview that was published in March 2018. You can listen to the full interview here, bit.ly/Sundaram_gender

FURTHER READING
- Ruth Golding on moving beyond narrow gendered roles, bit.ly/Goldingongender
- How teacher appellations reinforce gender inequality, bit.ly/SirandMiss
- The importance of teaching children about consent, bit.ly/Teaching_consent

Lightning Source UK Ltd.
Milton Keynes UK
UKHW020641110219
337094UK00009B/180/P

9 780995 741560